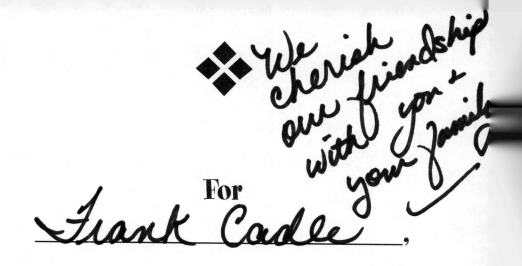

We cherish our friendship with you + your family!

For

Frank Cadle,

An Officially Excellent Dad

Martha Belton

from

Father's Day - 2004

date

OUR PURPOSE AT HOWARD PUBLISHING IS TO:

- *Increase faith* in the hearts of growing Christians
- *Inspire holiness* in the lives of believers
- *Instill hope* in the hearts of struggling people everywhere

BECAUSE HE'S COMING AGAIN!

Published by Howard Publishing Co., Inc.
3117 North 7th Street, West Monroe, Louisiana 71291-2227
www.howardpublishing.com

04 05 06 07 08 09 10 11 12 13   10 9 8 7 6 5 4 3 2 1

Edited by Between the Lines
Illustrations by Rex Bohn
Cover design by LinDee Loveland
Interior design by Stephanie D. Walker

Library of Congress Cataloging-in-Publication Data

Bolton, Martha, 1951–
    The "official" dad book : the who, what, when, where, why, and how of being a dad /
    Martha Bolton ; illustrated by Rex Bohn.
        p. cm.
    ISBN 1-58229-367-8 (clothbound) — ISBN 1-58229-368-6 (softcover)
    1. Fathers—Anecdotes. 2. Fathers—Humor. I Title.

HQ756.B65 2004
306.874'2—dc22

                                                                        2004040644

Scripture quotations not otherwise marked are taken from the HOLY BIBLE, NEW INTERNATIONAL VERSION ®. Copyright © 1973, 1978, 1984 by International Bible Society. Used by permission of Zondervan. All rights reserved. Scriptures marked NKJV are taken from the Holy Bible, New King James Version. Copyright © 1982 by Thomas Nelson, Inc.

Every reasonable effort has been made to trace the ownership of quoted material. We will gladly make corrections in future editions provided written notification is made to the publisher.

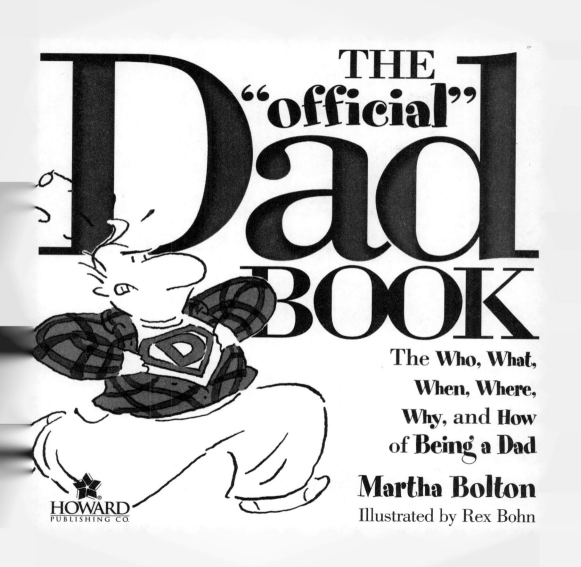

THE "official"

Dad

BOOK

The **Who, What,**
When, Where,
Why, and **How**
of **Being a Dad**

Martha Bolton

Illustrated by Rex Bohn

HOWARD
PUBLISHING CO.

A father's love makes you feel like you're on top of the world!

This book is dedicated to three special men in my life:

To my father, Lonnie, for his fatherly love, his dry wit, and for all the leftover desserts he brought home from the catering truck that would stop by the construction sites where he worked.

To my grandfather, Andrew, who used to take me for walks in the field and pick wildflowers and berries for me. I was just a young girl, but those walks are permanently etched in my memory. Granddads, you're important!

To my husband, Russ, who has been an amazingly encouraging, loving, teaching, faithful, defending, giving, fun father to our three sons. You've been there for them 100 percent of the time. In my biased opinion, there is no finer father.

Superdad! The king of the hill!

Contents

❖

Dads wrap you in love.

> **A truly rich man is one whose children run into his arms when his hands are empty.**
>
>
>
> **Author Unknown**

That's My Dad

From the beginning of man, dads have been there for their children. Even when they weren't quite sure what to do. Can you imagine what it must have been like when Adam first laid eyes on Cain, his firstborn son?

Adam and Eve had never seen a baby before. All sorts of thoughts must have been running through this new father's mind. Here are just a few comments Adam might have made to Eve.

- *What do you think it is?*

- *Well, I guess this explains your sudden weight gain.*

- *Try to think back. Maybe you ate something you shouldn't have . . . again.*

- *Please tell me he's not going to cry like that all night!*

- *Don't be ridiculous. If I had known that was trying to get out of you, of course I would have been more sympathetic to your pain!*

- *Wouldn't you know it . . . just when I get all the animals named, now I've gotta start naming these creatures.*

- *Look around. See if it came with instructions or something.*

- *So did you know this was going to happen, or are you just as surprised as I am?*

- *You're not going to have one of these every time you have a stomachache, are you?*

- *Is he going to be that little forever?*

- *Change him? What do you mean change him? He just got here. I like him the way he is. Why would I want to change him? . . . Oh, that.*

- *Aw . . . look at that smile. Kinda makes all the pain go away, doesn't it? OK, sorry—you're right, it's too soon. But one of these days, Eve, you're going to want to do this again. Trust me on this one.*

Whatever thoughts were running through Adam's head, we know one thing. He stepped up to the plate, and without any previous experience, without any how-to books, without any Lamaze classes, instructional videos, or mother-in-law lectures, without Dr. Laura, Dr. Spock, or even Dr. Seuss, Adam became a daddy. And from that day forth, dads have been doing their best to step up to the plate and be the best daddies they can be to their babies.

If the new American father feels bewildered and even defeated,

let him take comfort from the fact

that whatever he does in any fathering situation

has a 50 percent chance of being right.

Bill Cosby

Dad—the dragon slayer on the road of life.

THE **who** OF BEING A DAD

Not even the Kryptonite of football can stop him from coming to the rescue.

> **The child had every toy his father ever wanted.**
>
>
>
> **Robert C. Whitten**

Superdad

My husband still has the Superman outfit he wore when he was a little boy. One day one of our sons discovered it packed away in a box in our closet and thought he had uncovered a long-kept family secret—that his father was the real Superman!

For many children Dad is Superman. He's faster than a speeding baseball headed toward the neighbor's window, more powerful than the biggest bully, and able to leap over tall piles of toys in a single bound. They believe that just like Superman, Dad can do anything. Not even kryptonite could stop him from coming to the rescue of one of his little ones!

**My father gave me the greatest gift
anyone could give another person, he believed in me.**

Jim Valvano

Who Is a Dad?

A dad is easy to recognize.

He's the only guy on the beach wearing black socks.

He's the one crying when a blackout hits on Super Bowl Sunday.

He's the guy who takes an hour to explain something that could have been explained in two minutes by someone a lot less interested in whether you understand it.

He's the one standing over the barbecue putting out the blazing inferno that used to be hamburger patties.

At a basketball game, with less than two minutes left on the board (and the coach still hasn't put you in), he's the one cheering from the stands, saying "You're the best! Don't give up!"

My dad taught me to switch-hit.

He and my grandfather, who was left-handed,

pitched to me every day after school in the backyard.

I batted lefty against my dad and righty against my granddad.

Mickey Mantle

He opened the jar of pickles when no one else could . . .

When it rained, he got the car and brought it around to the door. When

anyone was sick, he went out to get the prescription filled. He took lots of

pictures . . . but he was never in them.

Erma Bombeck

It's only when you grow up, and step back from him,
or leave him for your own career and your own home—
it's only then that you can measure his greatness
and fully appreciate it. Pride reinforces love.

Margaret Truman

A fool despises his father's instruction,
but he who receives correction is prudent.
—Proverbs 15:5 NKJV

Who Is a Dad?. . .

He may not always get the respect he deserves.

He can be opinionated.

He can be a pushover.

He'll appreciate any gift you give him and wear it—including that blinking tie you bought last Christmas as a joke.

He'll appreciate any gift you give him—and wear it!

He can be stern.

He can make you feel special.

He makes time to listen.

He can be highly protective of his family, his politics, and his tools.

He can be unyielding when it comes to his favorite television shows.

He knows a lot of the answers to the questions on your homework.

He'll ride all the fun rides with you at amusement parks.

He believes you can be whatever you want to be.

He'll cushion your falls.

He understands.

He teases.

He encourages.

He holds you.

He loves you.

That's Dad.

**Father!
To God Himself we cannot give a holier name.**

William Wordsworth

Special Dads

Some dads are called upon to do special things—like be a father to some very special kids. Dr. Robert A. Naseef, author of *Special Children, Challenged Parents: The Struggles and Rewards of Raising a Child with a Disability*, quotes a few of these special dads in his writings:

> "Having a daughter with Down syndrome has changed my notion of what comprises a bad day. I appreciate life in such a different and more profound way."

> "I have learned to see past what my son (who has autism) isn't and focus on who he is. It takes time to find it in your heart."

> "I grew up without my father because my parents divorced when I

was very young. I was always determined to be there for my children. Now that I have two boys with special needs, they need me more than ever."

"I am a fixer, and I can't fix this. There is no wrench to pull out of my toolbox."

"My father had a horrible temper. I was determined to do better. My daughter's disability taught me such humility as I learned to accept what I could not change."

*Children show dads
how to look beyond the clouds.*

Dad, you take the prize!

**It is not flesh and blood,
but heart which makes us fathers and sons.**

Johann Friedrich Von Schiller

Adoptive Fathers

Adoptive dads are special dads too. My husband and I know firsthand the joy of adoption. As the adoptive parents of two of our three sons, we remember clearly the ecstatic joy of welcoming each of our sons into our family. It was with all the enthusiasm, all the pride, and all the love of any other parent. From the first moment a child bestows upon you the title of Dad, it doesn't matter how that child came into this world—you are bonded forever.

> *Whoever welcomes a little child like this
> in my name welcomes me.*
>
> —Matthew 18:5

Giving Credit Where Credit's Due

Famous Sons Speak Out

My best training came from my father.

Woodrow Wilson

I watched a small man with thick calluses on both hands work fifteen and sixteen hours a day . . . a man who came here uneducated, alone, unable to speak the language, who taught me all I needed to know about faith and hard work by the simple eloquence of his example.

Mario Cuomo

My dad has always taught me these words: care and share.

Tiger Woods

My dad was the force behind me early on.
He was just infatuated with baseball. He was the one that basically taught
me how to play the game. He gave a lot of his time working out with me,
practicing and taking me to a lot of different games.

Rafael Palmeiro

Dad taught me everything I know.
Unfortunately, he didn't teach me everything he knows.

Al Unser Jr.

I've never been jealous.
Not even when my dad finished the fifth grade
a year before I did.

Jeff Foxworthy

Famous Daughters Speak Out

I have always had the feeling I could do anything, and my dad told me I could. I was in college before I found out he might be wrong.

Ann Richards

*None of you can ever be proud enough of being the child
of such a Father who has not his equal in this world—
so great, so good, so faultless.
Try, all of you, to follow in his footsteps and don't be discouraged,
for to be really in everything like him, none of you,
I am sure, will ever be. Try, therefore, to be like him in some points,
and you will have acquired a great deal.*

Victoria, Queen of England

It doesn't matter who my father was;
it matters who I remember he was.

Anne Sexton

My father was a statesman,
I'm a political woman.
My father was a saint. I'm not.

Indira Gandhi

"Be like him in some points,
and you will have acquired
a great deal."

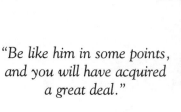

A dad is a lot of things.

THE what OF BEING A DAD

Children have more need of models, than of critics.

Joseph Joubert

Dads Are Examples

A dad is a lot of things, but mainly, he's an example. Children learn by watching. They watch their peers, the television, society, and they watch their parents. They may not copy everything they see, but they'll certainly copy some of it. Hopefully, what they copy will be those values we most want them to mimic.

Our children are watching us live,
and what we are
shouts louder than anything we can say.

Wilferd A. Peterson

Children have never been very good at listening to adults,

but they have never failed to imitate them.

James Baldwyn

Dads—the Michelangelo of the garage.

> It is easier to build strong children
> than to repair broken men.
>
>
>
> Frederick Douglas

Dads Are Builders

My father was a builder of things. He was a carpenter by trade, and he also loved building things around our house. One Christmas he made his own Christmas tree. I'm not talking about simply putting together an artificial tree that comes in a box. I'm talking about making a tree out of a broom handle and shrub branches.

It wasn't that we couldn't afford a Christmas tree. Dad was just bored and wanted something to do. And believe it or not, that tree ended up looking so much like a real tree, you would've had to look at its "trunk" to tell the difference.

My husband builds too. He's built patios, workbenches, a replica of an aircraft carrier for our sons to play with, and a lot more.

Dads like to build. They like to tinker in the garage. They like to create something amazing out of scrap pieces of lumber. The garage is their art gallery, their museum of endless endeavors.

But houses, workbenches, and even Christmas trees aren't the only things dads build. They also build character in their children. Generosity, loyalty, kindness, dependability, dedication to duty, and humility are just some of the important qualities that dads through the ages have tried to build in their children. And the world is a better place because of it.

Manual labor to my father was not only
good and decent for its own sake, but as he was given to saying,
it straightened out one's thoughts.

Mary Ellen Chase

Nothing is so strong as gentleness. Nothing is so gentle as real strength.

Frances de Sales

All the feeling which my father

could not put into words was in his hand—

any dog, child, or horse would recognize the kindness of it.

Freya Stark

You know, fathers just have a way
of putting everything together.

Erika Cosby

Dads Are Fixers

Dads fix things. Some of the things they fix may not have had anything wrong with them to begin with, but the majority of the time, a dad is a mender of the broken.

When I was a child, I believed my dad was nothing short of a miracle

Dads can fix anything.

worker. He could fix anything. My dad could also take a knickknack that had broken into dozens of pieces and, with the help of Elmer's glue, put the whole thing back together again. He was doing the crackled look in home decorating long before it became popular. I didn't

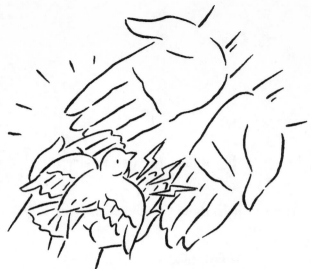

Even things that appear beyond hope can be mended by a dad.

worry if a toy broke, my bike chain fell off, or our tetherball broke free from the chain. All I had to do was gather up the broken parts and carry them to my dad, and within hours, the item would be as good as new.

My dad taught me a lot of things, but one of the most important things was that even when something appears damaged beyond any hope of repair, it can still be mended. It just takes a little extra work, perseverance, and faith.

Dads are bringers of hope.

If you talk to your children,

you can help them to keep their lives together.

If you talk to them skillfully,

you can help them to build future dreams.

Jim Rohn

Every hard knock they ever get

knocks the father even harder still, if that's possible,

and if and when they finally come through

more or less in one piece at the end,

there's maybe no rejoicing greater than his in all creation.

Frederick Buechner

*When I was a kid, I used to imagine animals
running under my bed. I told my dad,
and he solved the problem quickly. He cut the legs off the bed.*

❖

Lou Brock

Dads Are Defenders

Dads are natural defenders. They're our fortress, our safety net, our personal bodyguard on duty 24-7. Dads don't sleep. It might look like that's what they're doing when they're stretched out on their recliners, but be assured—it's a watchful sleep. (The snoring is just to throw us off.) Dads

never forget that they're the protector of the family, and at the slightest noise (or the changing of channels on the television set), these noble warriors will spring to life, ever ready to defend their offspring (or favorite TV program) with all the courage and strength they can muster.

Be assured—it's a watchful sleep.

No matter what his size, a father will unhesitatingly slay dragons and take on schoolyard bullies in his child's defense. Dads have been known to run into burning buildings, dive into angry waters, and even dash into speeding traffic to rescue their little ones from harm.

To put it bluntly, don't mess with a dad!

I cannot think of any need
in childhood as strong as the need for a father's protection.

Sigmund Freud

> **Beware of all enterprises that require new clothes.**
>
>
>
> **Henry David Thoreau**

Dads Are Fashion Confident

A father may not always be the coolest creature God ever created, but one thing you can say about a dad is that he's confident about who he is. Dads don't change with every new fashion trend that comes along. They are who they are, and they're fine with that. They love that old T-shirt that has more paint samples than a Home Depot. They're confident enough in their own fashion sense to ignore the dress code on a party invitation. (They interpret "formal attire" as "Get the grass stains off your jeans.")

When it comes to style, fathers are also fine with being fashionably late. Many dads tend to run about two seasons behind. My husband is a history buff, but frankly, I think he watches the history channel to get fashion tips.

Yet maybe Dad has the right idea. Maybe the rest of us are wrong. Maybe it is better to let fashion trends come and go and not get caught up in the hoopla. Maybe getting twenty-six years of wear out of those high-school sweatpants is a smart financial move. Maybe it's downright

Dad even wears the paint palette on his shirt so mom can find the perfect match.

genius to keep a paint palette on a T-shirt just in case you're ever out shopping and need to match the wall color with the upholstery on a new recliner. Maybe we've been trying to change the wrong person. Maybe Dad has the right look, and the rest of us need to get with *his* style.

If they want to see me, here I am.
If they want to see my clothes,
open my closet and show them my suits.

Albert Einstein

Fashion is a form of ugliness
so intolerable that we have to alter it every six months.

Oscar Wilde

Fashion is the science of appearances,

and it inspires one with the desire to seem rather than to be.

❖

Edwin Hubbel Chapin

Art produces ugly things which frequently become beautiful with time.

Fashion, on the other hand,

produces beautiful things which always become ugly with time.

❖

Jean Cocteau

Dad—the master of fashion.

> **What lies behind us and what lies before us are tiny matters compared to what lies within us.**
>
>
>
> **Ralph Waldo Emerson**

Dads Are Life Jackets

Nowhere did I appreciate my father more than in a swimming pool. My swimming skills were like the stock market. Sometimes I could stay afloat, but most of the time I was headed south fast.

Whenever my father saw me struggling in the water, he'd swim over to me and tell me to wrap my arms around him. He never made me get out of the pool just because I couldn't swim. He let me hang onto his neck

while he swam around, even venturing out into the deep end. He let me use his strength and skill to keep my head above water. And no matter how deep the water was, I never doubted that I was safe in his arms.

Dads can be there to help keep us afloat in the deep waters of life too. They're not there to hold us back and keep us from having fun by

Dads allow us to borrow their strength until we can swim off on our own.

making us get out of the pool. Instead, they allow us to borrow their strength and skill—to hang on as tightly as we need to until we're confident enough to swim off on our own.

I've been very blessed.
My parents always told me I could be anything I wanted.
When you grow up in a household like that,
you learn to believe in yourself.

Rick Schroeder

What Is Fatherhood?

It's learning
TO SHARE YOUR TOYS.

It's realizing
SOMEONE VERY DEPENDENT DEPENDS ON YOU.

It's a sense OF UNBELIEVABLE PRIDE OVER THE
SMALLEST OF ACCOMPLISHMENTS. ("LOOK! HE
CAN TOUCH HIS NOSE! DID
YOU SEE THAT?!")

It's being THE KNIGHT
IN SHINING ARMOR
TO A LITTLE PRINCESS.

It's having TO TEACH
ABOUT LIFE WHILE YOU'RE STILL
IN THE MIDDLE OF LEARNING ABOUT LIFE.

It's being STRONG WHEN
YOU FEEL WEAK.

It's trying
TO BE BRAVE
WHEN YOU'RE
MOST AFRAID.

It's being VULNERABLE.

It's doing EVERYTHING YOU CAN
TO COME THROUGH FOR SOMEONE.
("DAD, YOU GOT THE TICKETS! I THOUGHT THEY
WERE ALL SOLD OUT! YOU'RE THE BEST!")

It's taking
SIX PICTURES
OF THE SAME
EXPRESSION.

It's getting
TO PLAY BASEBALL AGAIN.

It's belly laughs OVER SILLY THINGS.

It's energizing.

It's exhausting.

WORLD'S BEST DAD!

It's rewarding.

It's exasperating.

It's expensive.

It's worth every cent.

It's loving SOMEONE MORE THAN YOU EVER THOUGHT YOU COULD LOVE ANYONE.

It can hurt REALLY BADLY AND FEEL REALLY WONDERFUL AT THE SAME TIME.

That's fatherhood.

You *are a father.*

I felt something impossible for me to explain in words.

Then when they took her away, it hit me.

I got scared all over again and began to feel giddy.

Then it came to me—I was a father.

Nat King Cole

Dads are dads all the time.

THE when OF BEING A DAD

*Dads come through
just in the nick of time.*

> **There's really no point in having children
> if you're not going to be home enough to be a father to them.**

Anthony Edwards

A Father's Arms Are Open 24-7

If you think rebellious children only came on the scene in modern times, think again. Two thousand years ago, Jesus told a parable about a son who turned his back on his father. For Him to use this story as an example, He must have known it would hit home with a lot of His audience.

In the story, the son asks his father for his inheritance ahead of time. In his adventurous nature, he didn't want to wait for it. He was a "gimme, gimme" child, and the father gave him what he wanted.

It didn't take long for the son to squander every last cent on wild living and end up at rock bottom. That's usually what happens when a child begs for something he's not mature enough to handle. But the son needed to learn his lesson. And he did. After ending up sharing a bed and breakfast with a pen full of pigs, the son remembered that even the servants at his father's house lived a whole lot better than he was at the moment; so he decided to return home. The young man didn't expect to be treated as a son. He knew he had given up any right to that. He would be content to be treated as a hired hand.

But what did this father do? The boy hadn't even reached the house yet when his father started running out to him. His dad threw his arms around him, kissed him, and then ordered his finest robe to be brought out and placed on him. He even threw a party!

No "I told you so's."

No "What in the world were you thinking?" sermons.

No twenty questions.

No weekly reminder afterward.

Just forgiveness.

And a big celebration.

That's a father's love.

Every parent is at some time the father

of the unreturned prodigal,

with nothing to do but keep his house open to hope.

John Ciardi

*He will turn the hearts
of the fathers to their children,
and the hearts of the children
to their fathers.*
—Malachi 4:6

When Do Children
No Longer Need a Father?

When life is perfect.

When hearts no longer break.

When disappointment is outlawed.

When there's nothing left to learn.

When falling no longer hurts.

When joy doesn't need to be shared.

When there's no more risk
of failure.

When feeling loved is no
longer important.

When do children no longer
need a father?

Never.

A boy is a magical creature. . . . When you come home at night with only

the shattered pieces of your hopes and dreams,

he can mend them like new with two magic words, "Hi, Dad!"

Alan Marshall Beck

The best inheritance a person

can give to his children is a few minutes of his time each day.

O. A. Battista

> **My father used to play with my brother and me in the yard.
> Mother would come out and say, "You're tearing up the grass."
> "We're not raising grass," my dad would reply, "we're raising boys."**

Harmon Killebrew

Dads Are Always Making Memories

My father wasn't an alcoholic. He didn't do drugs, gamble, or even smoke, for that matter. He did, however, have one addiction. My father was addicted to canned goods. No, that's not a typo. Every Friday night my dad would take his paycheck to Dale's grocery store, cash it, and go grocery shopping. My mother would leave work early just so she could load us kids into the car and go to find Dad before he could spend his entire earnings on canned mustard greens and peaches.

We usually got to the store just as Dad was filling his cart with Del Monte and Green Giant cans. I can picture it today as though it were yesterday—my dad putting the cans into the cart, my mother taking them out and putting them back on the shelf. He'd put them in, she'd take them out.

"You don't need those."

"Yes, I do."

"No, you don't."

"Move aside. I'm getting them."

"This is for your own good. We're putting them back."

It was like an intervention with a junkie, only Dad's craving was roughage.

Mom would eventually give in and let Dad keep some of the canned goods (you can't kick a mustard-green habit cold turkey), and looking back on it now, I'm inclined to think it was really more of a joke between them than anything. But it's one of my favorite memories. It seems making memories is one of the things dads do best.

Father, dear father, come home with me now,

The clock in the steeple strikes one;

You said you were coming right home from the shop,

As soon as your day's work was done.

Henry Clay Work

Words from Dads throughout History

George Washington's dad: You threw a dollar across the Potomac? What were you thinking, boy? Money doesn't grow on trees, you know!

Ben-Hur's dad: Don't make me pull this chariot over.

Picasso's dad: Of course I like your paintings, son. I'm just saying you might need to get your eyes checked. It's nothing to be embarrassed about. Lots of people wear glasses.

Napoleon's dad: I'm not playing games with you, Napoleon. Now take your hand out of your pocket and give me back the remote!

Albert Einstein's dad: You'll cut it if I say so! Now get in the car. We're going to the barber!

"Relatively shorter, please."

Rip Van Winkle's dad: Get up and go get a job. You gonna sleep your life away?

Ben Franklin's dad: You're acting like you've got no sense, boy. Now get that kite down, and get in out of the rain. All the neighbors are looking at you.

". . . now where did I put my key?"

John Glenn's dad: The moon? Can't you just go to a rock concert like other kids?

Genghis Khan's dad: You're just going to have to learn to get along with others.

Edgar Allen Poe's dad: Answer the door, Edgar, and quit telling me it's just a raven.

Mickey Mouse's dad: I know you're over fifty, son, but trust me, your voice will change. You've just got to be patient.

By the time a man realizes that maybe his father was right,
he usually has a son who thinks he's wrong.

Charles Wadsworth

Life was a lot simpler when what we honored was father and mother
rather than all major credit cards.

Robert Orben

I talk and talk and talk, and I haven't taught people in fifty years
what my father taught by example in one week.

Mario Cuomo

My father gave me free run of his library. When I think of my boyhood,
I think in terms of the books I read.

Jorge Luis Borges

My father didn't tell me how to live;

he lived

and let me watch him do it.

Clarence B. Kelland

A father helps you reach new heights.

Dads Lift Us Up

When we can't reach the cookie jar.

When we want to see what's over the fence.

When the water's too deep.

When we're too tired to stand on our own.

When we want a toy on the top shelf.

When we've fallen and need help getting up.

When we need a shoulder to cry on.

When we want to feel safe.

When we just want to be in his arms.

Dads are easy to find.

THE where

OF BEING A

DAD

Where's Dad? Just follow the trail.

**Cleaning your house while your kids are still growing
is like shoveling the walk before it stops snowing.**

Phyllis Diller

Along the Sock Trail

Where's Dad? Perhaps we should begin with looking at where he's been. With some dads its easy to tell. Just follow the trail of dirty socks, T-shirts, shoes, and the sports section of the previous week's newspaper on the floor. It's not that dads want to be messy. It's just that there's something inside them that seems to date back to earlier days when a dad would go hunting for dinner, leaving a trail behind to aid his loved ones in finding him should he not return to the homestead.

Granted, the chances of a dad today getting lost on the way to the bedroom, the kitchen, or even the family room are slim; but his instinct is still to leave a trail. Perhaps those dirty socks are a dad's message to the world. They say, "I've been here. I existed. I have walked these carpets and vinyl floors, and I have stories to tell."

The message of a tidy mom might be "I have cleaned. I have vacuumed. I have no stories to tell because I am exhausted."

But Dad? His tales are right there where everyone will be sure to trip over them. The world has to notice his existence.

It could be, then, that keeping everything in its place isn't as important as some think it is. Maybe it's more important to live life, enjoy our families to the fullest, and make sure we're leaving a long trail of wonderful stories behind us.

Man is made for something better than disturbing dirt.

Oscar Wilde

At the worst, a house unkept cannot be so distressing as a life unlived.

Rose Macaulay

THE DAD WEARABILITY TEST:

Have you ever taken anything out of the clothes basket

because it had become, relatively, the cleaner thing?

Katharine Whitehorn

A dad's idea of heaven.

> **If a man watches three football games in a row,**
> **he should be declared legally dead.**

Erma Bombeck

Remote Fathers

One place you're likely to find a dad is in front of the television. A dad loves to sit in a recliner (or turn the sofa into one) and watch TV. Especially sports. The size of the ball doesn't matter. It can be a football, a basketball, a baseball, a soccer ball, a golf ball, a tennis ball, or even a bowling ball—dads love watching sports programs.

They even watch shows about sports programs. They'll watch the pregame show, the halftime show, the postgame show, the week's highlights, and the season wrap-up. They'll watch the live game, the instant replays, and the sports analysis. Dads will watch their games on the networks, cable, satellite, and the Internet. The games they miss (because they're watching other games), they'll record on their VCRs, DVDs, or TiVo.

Dad's world revolves around sports.

When they're not watching sports, dads are talking sports. They'll talk about the games at work, in the parking lot after church, over coffee with friends, and with their neighbors. They'll telephone their friends or exchange e-mails. They'll relive past games and speculate on future ones.

There's no getting around it—dads love sports.

But moms enjoy sports too. Especially wrestling. The kind that happens when she tries to get the remote control out of Dad's hand.

You've got to be very careful if you don't know where you're going, because you might not get there.

Yogi Berra

In Training

Maybe one of the reasons dads love watching sports so much is all the life lessons that can be learned from them—lessons dads are more than willing to pass down to future generations.

All winning teams are goal-oriented. Teams like these win consistently because everyone connected with them concentrates on specific objectives. They go about their business with blinders on; nothing will distract them from achieving their aims.

Lou Holtz

I've missed more than 9,000 shots in my career.
I've lost more than 300 games. Twenty-six times I've been trusted to take
the game-winning shot and missed. I've failed over and over
and over again in my life. . . . And that is why I succeed.

Michael Jordan

You've got to play with your heart, with every fiber of your body.
If you're lucky enough to find a guy with a lot of head and a lot of heart,
he's never going to come off the field second.

Vince Lombardi

There are three types of baseball players: those who make it happen, those
who watch it happen, and those who wonder what happens.

Tommy Lasorda

A leader has to know his job. If you want people to follow you, you have to know where you are going.

Joe Namath

The more I practice, the luckier I get.

Arnold Palmer

Fishing is about spending time together.

> **Fishing is much more than fish. It is the great occasion when we may return to the fine simplicity of our forefathers.**

Herbert Hoover

Gone Fishing

If you don't find Dad in front of the TV watching sports and learning about life, you might want to check the local fishing hole. Whether it's for bass, rockfish, tarpin, marlin, tuna, or trout, lots of dads enjoy the challenge of trying to land the big one. (Or at least get bragging rights about the one that got away.) These same dads who can hardly drag themselves out of bed during the week will get up before dawn on a Saturday morning because that's when the fish are biting.

Dads love to fish for a number of reasons. For some it brings back memories of fishing with their father. For others the peacefulness of fishing is the draw. You can't be in a rush. Fishing is about slowing down long enough to see the scenery, quieting down enough to hear the silence, and relaxing enough to appreciate them both.

When our sons were younger, my husband used to take them fishing on a regular basis. Those trips were a special time of bonding—and photo opportunities. We have scores of pictures of each of the boys with their first fish. And for one of the boys, we have something more.

My husband decided that this prize catch was worthy of more than a mere photo. This fish, according to my husband, deserved to be mounted. He was going to stuff the little guy (the fish, not our son), mount it to some wood, and hang it on the wall of our home.

Now on the surface, mounting a first fish might seem like a nice thing for a dad to do. But you have to understand, my husband is no taxidermist. Nor did he intend to call one. His plan was to mount this fish himself and "save us a fortune" (four words that have been striking fear in the hearts of wives for centuries).

He gutted the fish but was disappointed with how scrawny it looked. It wasn't a particularly large fish to begin with, but filleted, it looked even smaller. So he decided to try to bring the fish back to its former self by stuffing it . . . with newspaper. The wrinkled wads of the *Los*

Angeles Times gave the fish a lumpy exterior, but even that didn't wane my husband's enthusiasm for his project.

Next came the sealer. His only experience with decoupage had been the credit-card plaque he made one year by cutting all our credit cards in half and making a plaque out of them. Credit cards, fish, what's the difference, he figured. They both involve a hook you don't always see. But I digress.

My husband took the brush and applied coat after coat after coat of lacquer to the fish, securing it in place. That fish wasn't going any-where. It looked a little like a relief map, but my husband was beaming

THANKS, DAD!

Dad decided that this prize catch was worthy of more than a mere photo.

with pride and accomplishment when he finally presented it to our son. And our son beamed right back. He couldn't believe it. His prize fish was there on a plaque for all the world to see.

And smell. Apparently, decoupage doesn't lock in the aroma of a rotting fish. For years, when people came to our house, they would ask if I had been cooking fish. Before I could answer, their next question was "If you are, you'd better check the freshness date."

Our son is twenty-seven years old now, and he still has that fish. It withered some more, even under all that glue, but I'm happy to say that after nearly two decades, it has finally stopped stinking.

Like they say, it's the thought that counts.

Ten years from now I plan to be sitting here, looking out over my land.
I hope I'll be writing books, but if not,
I'll be on my pond fishing with my kids.
I feel like the luckiest guy I know.

John Grisham

If people concentrated on the really important things in life,
there'd be a shortage of fishing poles.

Doug Larson

When it's over, I'm going home to Mobile and fish for a long time.

Hank Aaron

It is admirable for a man to take his son fishing,

but there is a special place in heaven

for the father who takes his daughter shopping.

John Sinor

Fishing for Truths

Like other sports, fishing can teach a dad a lot about life too.

To climb a tree to catch a fish is talking much and doing nothing.

Chinese Proverb

*Chance is always powerful. Let your hook be always cast;
in the pool where you least expect it, there will be a fish.*

Ovid

*Many men go fishing their entire lives
without knowing it is not fish they are after.*

Henry David Thoreau

The man-versus-meat challenge dates back to when dads had to get their dinner with a spear instead of a debit card.

> To the old saying that man built the house but woman made of it a "home" might be added the modern supplement that woman accepted cooking as a chore but man has made of it a recreation.

Emily Post

Shall We Gather at the Barbecue?

Another place dads tend to spend a lot of time is at the barbecue. Dads love grilling. Maybe it's the man-versus-meat challenge that dates back to when hunters had to get their dinner with a spear or musket instead of a debit card. Whatever drives men to barbecue, on any given weekend, you can see the smoke plume from thousands of barbecues all across the land rising to the sky in a sort of tribal signal to other fathers, saying "Peace. Blessings. And the burgers are done."

*On any given weekend, you can see smoke
from barbecues rising in a tribal signal between fathers.*

Dad's Barbecuing Guide:

Rare:
WHY WON'T THIS FIRE START?

Medium:
I WONDER HOW MUCH
LIGHTER FLUID I
SHOULD USE.

Well:
DIDN'T I USED TO
HAVE EYEBROWS?

Dads add fun to the lives of their children.

THE why OF BEING A DAD

Dads help bring life into balance.

> **Most American children
> suffer too much mother and too little father.**
>
>
>
> **Gloria Steinem**

Dads Matter

Dads matter. A dad can help provide balance and stability in a child's life. He can be one more reassuring voice saying that no matter what the crisis of the day is, everything is going to turn out all right. A dad can be another set of ears to listen or one more shoulder to lean on. He can add fun to the lives of his children. He's the other half of his children's heritage—one who can remind them of the joys of their past and help them look forward to their future.

Dads are important.

There are very good reasons for Dad to be there. . . .

They roughhouse, they tease, they help you deal with

your frustrations, they don't always gratify your needs

in the way you want, and yet this can help you feel that you're

going to be OK when you're apart from your Mommy.

Kyle Pruett

Why Be There?

Be there for their sake.

A baby is born with a need to be loved—
and never outgrows it.

Frank A. Clark

Children need love,
especially when they do not deserve it.

Harold Hulbert

Be there for your sake.

When you become a parent, it is your biggest chance to grow again.

You have another crack at yourself. Parents are like shuttles on a loom.

They join the threads of the past with the

threads of the future and leave their own

bright patterns as they go.

❖

Fred Rogers

Of all nature's gifts to the human race,
what is sweeter to a man than his children?

Marcus Cicero

You can learn many things from children.
How much patience you have, for instance.

Franklin P. Jones

Fathers, like mothers, are not born. Men grow into fathers
—and fathering is a very important stage in their development.

David M. Gottesman

As for my father, few souls are less troubled. He can be simply pleased with us, pleased that we exist, and, from the vantage point of his wondrously serene old age, he contemplates our lives almost as if they were books he can dip into whenever he wants.

❖

Angela Carter

Dad's delight in their children's lives.

Be there for fun's sake.

The great man is he who does not lose his child's heart.

Mencius

A child reminds us that playtime is an essential part of our daily routine.

Anonymous

Be there for the future's sake.

What can you do to promote world peace?

Go home and love your family.

Mother Teresa

The words that a father speaks to his children in the privacy of home
are not heard by the world, but, as in whispering-galleries,
they are clearly heard at the end and by posterity.

Jean Paul Richter

Sometimes the poorest man leaves his children the richest inheritance.

Ruth E. Renkel

Perhaps the greatest social service that can be rendered by anybody to the
country and to mankind is to bring up a family.

George Bernard Shaw

There is always a moment in childhood
when the door opens and lets the future in.

Graham Greene

Be there for revenge's sake.

There are few things more satisfying

than seeing your children have teenagers of their own.

❖

Doug Larson

Be there because you're their hero.

No one knows the true worth of a man but his family.
The dreary man drowsing, drop-jawed, in the commuter train . . .
may be the pivot of a family's life,
welcomed with hugs, . . . asked for advice.

Pam Brown

Being a Dad Is Not for the Weak

Raising kids is part joy and part guerilla warfare.

Ed Asner

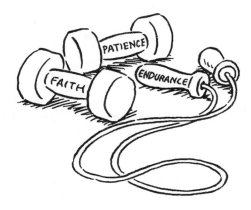

Having a family is like having a bowling alley installed in your brain.

Martin Mull

*Childhood is that wonderful time of life
when all you need to do to lose weight is take a bath.*

Richard Zera

*Children are a great comfort in your old age—
and they help you reach it faster too.*

Lionel Kauffman

*Children really brighten up a household.
They never turn the lights off.*

Ralph Bus

The face of a child can say it all, especially the mouth part of the face.

Jack Handey

The age of your children is a key factor in how quickly

you are served in a restaurant. We once had a waiter in Canada

who said, "Could I get you your check?"

and we answered, "How about the menu first?"

Erma Bombeck

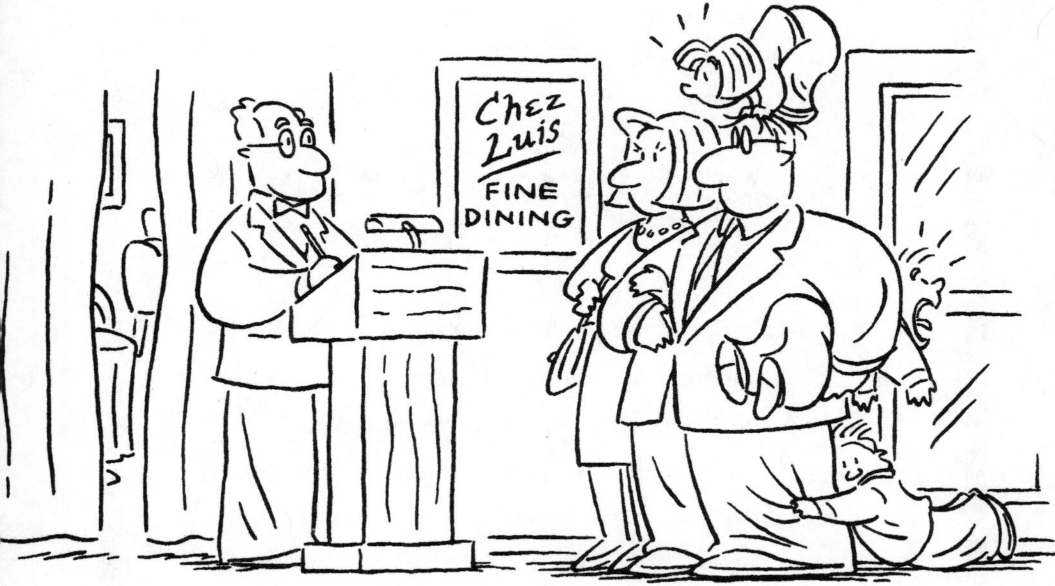
Chez Luis
FINE DINING

It Was Hard Even for God

For God so loved the world that he gave his one and
only Son, that whoever believes in him
shall not perish but have eternal life.
For God did not send his Son into the world to con-
demn the world, but to save the world through him.
—John 3:16–17

The LORD looks down from heaven on the sons of men to see if there are any who understand, any who seek God.

—Psalm 14:2

How great is the love the Father has lavished on us, that we should be called children of God!

—1 John 3:1

He was pierced for our transgressions, he was crushed for our iniquities; the punishment that brought us peace was upon him, and by his wounds we are healed.

—Isaiah 53:5

Father Really Does Know Best

On Adversity

All the adversity I've had in my life, all my troubles and obstacles, have strengthened me. . . . You may not realize it when it happens, but a kick in the teeth may be the best thing in the world for you.

Walt Disney

On Public Speaking

My father gave me these hints on speech-making:
"Be sincere . . . be brief . . . be seated."

James Roosevelt

On Friendship

My father always used to say that when you die,
if you've got five real friends, then you've had a great life.

Lee Iacocca

On Politics

You can't be in politics unless you can walk in a room
and know in a minute who's for you and who's against you.

Samuel E. Johnson

On Careers

My father always told me, "Find a job you love
and you'll never have to work a day in your life."

Jim Fox

On Business

My father said: "You must never try to make all the money that's in a deal.
Let the other fellow make some money too, because if you have a reputation
for always making all the money, you won't have many deals."

J. Paul Getty

On Perseverance

Strength does not come from winning. Your struggles develop your strengths.
When you go through hardships and decide not to surrender, that is strength.

Arnold Schwarzenegger

On Hard Work

My father taught me to work; he did not teach me to love it.

I never did like to work, and I don't deny it. I'd rather read,

tell stories, crack jokes, talk, laugh—anything but work.

Abraham Lincoln

On Everything

When I was a boy of fourteen, my father was so ignorant I could hardly

stand to have the old man around. But when I got to be twenty-one,

I was astonished at how much the old man had learned in seven years.

Mark Twain

THE
how
OF BEING A
DAD

A Father's-Day gift dad can really use.

Govern a family as you would cook a small fish—very gently.

Chinese Proverb

The Play Book

So how do you be a dad? Is there a rule book? A coach? A personal trainer? Should you read every how-to book on the market and follow each suggestion to the letter? Should you follow the example of your own dad, who might have followed the example of his dad, who could have followed the example of his dad? How can you study enough to know all the answers to all the questions your children are going to ask? How do you know which boundaries should be firm and which should have some flexibility? How do you be a friend to your children without losing parental authority? How in the world, in today's pressure-filled, me-first society, do you be a dad?

The answer is simple—one step, one lesson, one hug, one conversation, one memory at a time.

A king, realizing his incompetence, can either delegate
or abdicate his duties. A father can do neither.
If only sons could see the paradox, they would understand the dilemma.

Marlene Dietrich

The more people have studied different methods of bringing up children the
more they have come to the conclusion that what good mothers and fathers
instinctively feel like doing for their babies is the best after all.

Benjamin Spock

When my kids become wild and unruly,
I use a nice safe playpen. When they're finished, I climb out.

Erma Bombeck

Before I was married, I had a hundred theories about raising children and no children. Now, I have three children and no theories.

John Wilmot

Our children are here to stay, but our babies and toddlers

and preschoolers are gone as fast as they can grow up—

and we have only a short moment with each.

When you see a grandfather take a baby in his arms,

you see that the moment hasn't always been long enough.

St. Clair Adams Sullivan

Qualities of a Good Father

Dads Teach

One father is more than a hundred

schoolmasters.

George Herbert

A man who gives his children
habits of industry
provides for them better than by giving them
a fortune.

Richard Whately

Dads Lead

The responsibility of a man is to lead his family.

Ezra Taft Benson

He was, from the beginning, the unchallenged head of our household.
Any man I could override wouldn't hold my interest for long.

Minnie Pearl

Dads Make Time

A man should never neglect his family for business.

Walt Disney

If we are going to make a difference as fathers,

we need to do it now. The decision is practical.

It has to do with bedtimes, Saturday football games, stories,

and hamburgers; and it has to do with

carving those times out of busy lives—today.

Rob Parsons

GRUMPH   FRUMPTH   ARHGR

Dads Communicate

My heart is happy, my mind is free.

I had a father who talked with me.

Hilda Bigelow

We spend the first twelve months

of our children's lives teaching them to walk

and talk and the next twelve

telling them to sit down and shut up.

Phyllis Diller

Dads Ask

You know your children are growing up when they stop asking you where

they came from and refuse to tell you where they are going.

P. J. O'Rourke

Dads Discipline

Any child can tell you that the sole purpose of a middle name

is so he can tell when he's really in trouble.

Dennis Fakes

There are three ways to get something done:

do it yourself, employ someone,

or forbid your children to it.

Monta Crane

Anyone who thinks the art of conversation is dead

ought to tell a child to go to bed.

❖

Robert Gallagher

Dads Adjust

Everything in my life is now more moist. Between your spittle,
your diapers, your spit-up and drool, you got your baby food,
your wipes, your formula, your leaky bottles, sweaty baby backs,
and numerous other untraceable sources—all creating an ever-present
moistness in my life, which heretofore was mainly dry.

Paul Reiser

Dads Know What's Important

I have found out in later years that my family was very poor,

but the glory of America is that we didn't know it.

❖

Dwight D. Eisenhower

In the final analysis it is not what you do for your children
but what you have taught them to do for themselves
that will make them successful human beings.

❖

Ann Landers

Teaching children to do for themselves makes them successful human beings.

Dads Pay the Price

Insomnia: A contagious disease often transmitted from babies to parents.

Shannon Fife

There are times when parenthood seems nothing more

than feeding the hand that bites you.

Ann Diehl

Dads Advise

I have found that the best way to give advice

to your children is to find out what they want

and then advise them to do it.

Harry S. Truman

Dads Sacrifice

I've had a hard life, but my hardships are nothing against the hardships that my father went through in order to get me to where I started.

Bartrand Hubbard

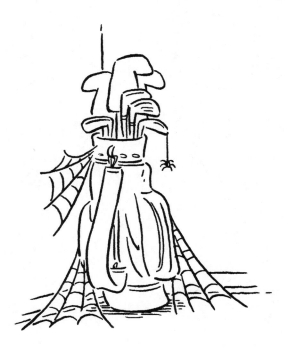

Dads Hope

My hope for my children must be that they respond to the still, small voice of God in their own hearts.

Andrew Young

Dads Endure

No matter what stage your child is in,

the parents who have older children

always tell you the next stage is worse.

Dave Barry

People who say they sleep like a baby usually don't have one.

Leo J. Burke

*Teenagers are people who act like babies
if they're not treated like adults.*

MAD Magazine

*Many a man wishes he were strong enough to tear
a telephone book in half—especially if he has a teenage daughter.*

Guy Lombardo

Dads Set Boundaries

The persons hardest to convince

that they're at the retirement age are children at bedtime.

Shannon Fife

Dads believe their children can do anything.

Dads Make Us Believe
We Can Do Anything

All kids need is a little help,
a little hope and somebody who believes in them.

Earvin "Magic" Johnson

How great is the love the Father has lavished on us,
that we should be called children of God!
—1 John 3:1

The best portion of a good man's life is his little,
nameless, unremembered acts of kindness and of love.

William Wordsworth

The Perfect Father

If we want to see an example of the perfect Father, we only have to look up. When it comes to fatherhood, God sets the standard. In fact, if you read the Bible, you'll find even God saying (or implying) some popular Dad-isms.

To see the perfect Father, look up.

Popular Dad-isms

Sit still!

Be still, and know that I am God;
I will be exalted among the nations,
I will be exalted in the earth.
—Psalm 46:10

**You can borrow my things,
but I expect you to take care of them.**

*The LORD God took the man and put him in the Garden of Eden
to work it and take care of it.*

—Genesis 2:15

Money doesn't grow on trees, you know.

Of what use is money in the hand of a fool,
since he has no desire to get wisdom?

—Proverbs 17:16

Sometimes you've gotta stand up to bullies.

As the Philistine moved closer to attack him,
David ran quickly toward the battle line to meet him.
Reaching into his bag and taking out a stone, he slung it
and struck the Philistine on the forehead.
The stone sank into his forehead,
and he fell facedown on the ground.
—1 Samuel 17:48–49

Now, say you're sorry.

I am happy, not because you were made sorry,
but because your sorrow led you to repentance.
—2 Corinthians 7:9

Don't make me have to say this again!

Remember the day you stood before the LORD your God . . .
when he said to me, "Assemble the people before me to hear my words
so that they may learn to revere me as long as they live in the land
and may teach them to their children."

—Deuteronomy 4:10

Understanding "Dad Speak"

Having trouble being understood? Here's a list to help your loved ones interpret the native language of most dads—grunting.

Umph: WHERE'S DINNER?

Hmpfh: TOUCH THAT REMOTE AND YOU'RE OUT OF THE WILL!

Grrr: SO THIS IS THE GUY YOU'RE GOING OUT WITH TONIGHT? SAVE THE MIDDLE SEAT FOR ME.

Don't touch that remote!

Grumph: YOU CAN'T HAVE A RAISE IN YOUR ALLOWANCE UNTIL YOUR MOTHER GIVES ME A RAISE IN MY ALLOWANCE.

Save the middle seat for me!

Arhgr: YOUR PRINCIPAL WANTS TO MEET WITH ME TOMORROW. I DON'T SUPPOSE HE WANTS TO TELL ME YOU'RE VALEDICTORIAN?

Frumpth: GET A HAIRCUT!

Yeowwww: HOW MANY TIMES HAVE I TOLD YOU NOT TO LEAVE YOUR SKATEBOARD IN THE MIDDLE OF THE LIVING ROOM? WE'RE GOING TO TALK ABOUT THIS JUST AS SOON AS I LAND!

Ahhh: REALLY? A HUG FOR NO REASON? WHAT'D I DO TO DESERVE A GREAT KID LIKE YOU?

"We'll talk about this as soon as I land . . ."

Dads come in different shapes, sizes, ages, and occupations—
but they all love their children.

The Last Word on Being a Dad

It's not easy to sum up the importance of a dad. I've tried in these few pages to cover some of the things Dad is, but he's so much more. Even when he's yelling, "Yoohoo, sweetie, you forgot your retainer!" from across a crowded junior high school campus, even when he interrogates your date or tries to act cool with your friends by saying something is "radirific," dads are special.

Dads come in all shapes, sizes, ages, and occupations. They have varying interests. Some are football fans. Others prefer baseball. Some live, eat, and breathe golf. Others prefer to spend their relaxing time in front of the television. Some fathers are funny. Others are serious. Some have lots of money. Others are just making it from paycheck to paycheck. Some are biological fathers. Others are adoptive fathers.

As different as dads can be, one thing that millions of them throughout history have had in common is an unwavering love for their children.

And for millions of children, young or grown, the feeling is mutual.

Father's Day Gift Ideas

ANKLE MODEL

Retractable Remote Control

The Retractable Remote Control is always attached to its base via a retractable wire. When someone takes the remote, it will automatically snap back to its rightful home. The base can be attached to an easy chair, couch, or coffee table. Wrist and ankle models are also available.

Football Season Alarm Clock

Imagine an alarm clock that will only wake you during football season. Why should grizzly bears get to hibernate and not man? Bears don't have to put up with cranky bosses, manipulative coworkers, or telemarketers. All they do is catch fish, look for honey, and dig through a few trash cans. So if you think sleeping through every season but football is a good idea, drop the hint for this unique Father's Day gift. (There's even a snooze alarm for those who only care to awake for the play-offs!)

Golfer's Wet Suit

Hate it when you have to go for a swim to find that lost golf ball? Well, this new item won't improve your game, but it'll sure help keep you dry and more comfortable. Fits neatly in your golf bag. Available in S, M, L, and XL, and in a variety of colors.

Wallet Alarm

It's worked for cars, houses, and other valuable possessions. So why not have an alarm for your wallet? Just set the alarm and don't worry about anyone getting into your wallet without your knowledge. If anyone gets too close, the alarm will sound. Equally effective on muggers, wives, and teenagers.

Medal of Valor for Dads

Presented to

_____

on this day of

_____

in recognition of his attention to duty, unselfish sacrifice,
and outstanding achievement in the following areas:

Check all that apply.

❑ Changing _____ diapers to date

❑ Waiting up _____ nights for teenagers to get home

❑ Driving _____ miles picking up children at sports, music, or
church activities

❑ Listening to countless rehearsals and recitals of the following
instruments: _____
_____

❑ Attending _____ baseball, football, soccer, basketball, bowling,
and tennis practices and games

- ❑ Meeting with scores of teachers, principals, pastors, and youth workers in regard to child's progress
- ❑ Defending against _____ bullies
- ❑ Counseling _____ hours
- ❑ Tutoring _____ hours
- ❑ Donating well over $_____ for the health, education, well-being, and happiness of the following children: _____
  _____
- ❑ Other: _____
  _____

This Medal of Valor is being awarded to the above named exceptional dad, who has gone above and beyond the call of duty, has risen to the challenge, and has overcome every obstacle that has come his way.

Signature _____

Witness _____

Date _____

certified • certified • certified • certified

with love

❖ Remote Control ❖

**Bearer is entitled to the unquestioned control
of the remote for the period of twenty-four hours.**

*Others in the household will watch the Discovery Channel, the History
Channel, sports programs, programs about sports programs, and various
news programs without grumbling, complaining, or attempts at interception.*

❖ Free Pass ❖

**Bearer is entitled to one free pass from department-store
or mall shopping.**

*Nontransferable. Other dads will need to buy
their own copy of this book for their coupon.*

❖ R & R ❖

**Bearer shall receive a three-day vacation
in the recliner of his choice.**

❖ Super Bowl Viewing ❖
Bearer is entitled to one uninterrupted
viewing of a Super Bowl game.

"Interruptions" include but are not limited to vacuuming, children fighting,
dogs barking, and questions such as "Which teams are playing?"
"Who's got the ball?" and "How many innings are left?"

❖ Free Pass ❖
Bearer is entitled to one free pass on mowing the lawn.

During this period, should any person or persons wander onto the lawn
and disappear in the thick brush, emergency workers shall be summoned.
Under no circumstances is the bearer of this coupon
to be disturbed until this rest period has passed.

❖ T-Shirt Preservation ❖
Bearer may select one T-shirt for protection
in the National Historical Registry.

We never know the love of our parents
for us till we have become parents.

Henry Ward Beecher

What you have inherited from your father, you must earn over again for
yourselves, or it will not be yours.

Johann Wolfgang von Goethe

Blessed indeed is the man
who hears many gentle voices call him father!

Lydia M. Child

One of life's greatest mysteries is how the boy who wasn't good enough

to marry your daughter can be the father

of the smartest grandchild in the world.

❖

Jewish Proverb

The smartest grandchild in the world.

Dad—you are special. You are amazing. You are loved.